a slice from the cake made of air

# *a* slice from the *cake* made of *air*

## Lillian-Yvonne Bertram

Red Hen Press | *Pasadena, CA*

Book layout by Hannah Nelson & Latina Vidolova

Library of Congress Cataloging-in-Publication Data

Names: Bertram, Lillian-Yvonne, 1983– author.
Title: A slice from the cake made of air / Lillian-Yvonne Bertram.
Description: First edition. | Pasadena, CA : Red Hen Press, [2016]
Identifiers: LCCN 2015046618 | ISBN 9781597093415 (softcover)
Subjects: | BISAC: POETRY / General.
Classification: LCC PS3602.E7685 A6 2016 | DDC 811/.6—dc23
LC record available at http://lccn.loc.gov/2015046618

The National Endowment for the Arts, the Los Angeles County Arts Commission, the Los Angeles Department of Cultural Affairs, the Dwight Stuart Youth Fund, the Pasadena Arts & Culture Commission and the City of Pasadena Cultural Affairs Division, the Ahmanson Foundation, and Sony Pictures Entertainment partially support Red Hen Press.

First Edition
Published by Red Hen Press
www.redhen.org

# acknowledgments

The author gratefully acknowledges the publishers of the journals and anthologies in which some of these poems first appeared: *Abjective*: "Dialogical Repose in Which I am the Magician's Most Trusted Girl," "Pastiche Eclogue," "A Village Life"; *Anti-*: "Personal Science Tracing as a Bear in the Lake on the Sun"; *Gulf Coast*: "Animals Do Not Commit Delusional Acts"; *Subtropics*: "Activation Energy," "Hungry Like Red"; *Vinyl*: "Clinical Therapy," "Sometimes I ask to be bound," "Strip District Eclogue."

Some of these poems appeared in the chapbook *cutthroat glamours*, winner of the 2012–2013 Phantom Books chapbook contest.

# contents

*n*

*r*

at intervals never when the moon is blue

a slice from the cake made of air

*r*

**Sometimes I ask to be bound**

But we
never do it like that.
Why don't we
ever do it
like that

After all
I ask for it

From my father anything
I ask for

I get

I say I am worth it
& we both know it's true.

      We know
there is a pattern
The chimney    In the rat's

nest

The leak always starts
above

I ask for me

                    I want
a mask the width of a rope   The
sky

moony memories

and the cut
of them

By this writing
you'd think
I wasn't born anywhere—

that I didn't however briefly
uncarry a child

Here
comes the scything

We know there is a pattern

Now the staining

Why can't we do it like that

With the taste
of mushrooms in the air

*n*

## Clinical Therapy

Dreaming again of an effortless

brother. He estranges me
with a plastic orange sword.

Pirates at play are we? Or
hawking through a forest. *Step carefully, step*

*carefully.* A car

passes. Do we even think who our father
will teach to drive

first? *Double dare, double*

*dare.* Never, no never. A cloud transforms
from shoe

& back again. All
that wasn't allowed comes back again.

It's the year I repeat
haircuts from the year

I wanted to be a boy.

No thought to what I would become:
cagey

bitch flicking photograph after photograph
with all the practice

of a trick punch. No stranger
to that feeling of bearing down

*bearing down.*

Activation Energy

## [de novo]

in which, from scratch, we design the big picture: one catalyst firecracking the vessels into life, into flesh—in which the flesh can die of the hiccups, a case in which the survival rate for an occurrence in the esophagus is one hundred percent—and what a world it is to suck in air and release with it a song as does a man crossing through the woods tonight, or to detect the end that blood comes to in the neck of the rabbit in the jaw of the cat—where one function surrounds and operates upon another like a sleeve to enhance not the heart but the willful glands that when catalyzed, do what the heart muscle calls upon us to do when it wants what it wants, in which we are suspended in water, tears, earwax, and the simple sugars and citrus spermidine of the prostate that are sour to the tongue—in which with the tongue there is no trying to taste as there is trying to apprehend sound with the ear, wherein the tongue is a muscle built solely for perception, in which we solubilize in the sweetness of substrate & enzyme—it is much more than "tab A into slot B," or a lock fit to its key—it is your process which I surround in my hands, that which is alive and into it I stroke more life

## [ab initio]

## Dialogical Repose in Which I am
## the Magician's Most Trusted Girl

At the height of prime time.  Just then

grinding out orgasm. Grinding out pendular

stroke, stoking literally—the insider

element, silicone in bathhouse décor.

*Takeittome* blue.     A task that poses no real danger.

Since. Forcing. Forcing my little hen further.

This isn't a real orgasm, a real patellar fatigue.

Is done with the boys I say, I say on to the mine,

on to the ghost,  splurge the forgot town.

On to the filler the spiller the shine

the mitten the bitten the rumpus the rind.

The rumpus the rind the bitten begot.  Got

was the way I took to the sequin, the hill.

The homestead was a blanket in thigh-cinch.

My cinch, my dappled Appaloosa on head

My mutton chop   My mother lode   My talents

are crowning   The crow is groaning   The pigeons

electric & guiltless & freed   What are those mountains

so wildly seen? Before me *los padres*   the fathers   the swine.

Into the canyon, the boxed horse I climb.

# The Organism Is Escaping

*Abstract*

What *we* call the body is a team of organs called the organism culled by organs pushing against the topographical surface. To the baby the mother says so there is skin by her touching and there is no body until the mother is touching and in touching she seals and so, she says, so there is a border, a seal, a limit without skin a cover without seam. It is the skin. The sounds of the animal indicate the animal to the animal, indicate the limit of the animal to the animal, the border, the crossing of the breath: I end here with my breath. Hear, end with my breath. Hear end with my breath, my breath of body, my machine desiring, my lung extending out my body through my breath the bubble. Through borderless breath the coypu the macaw the baby extends its border, its seal, its flesh the border of the body, the wall, the sponge, the surface, flesh and nerve. Flesh and nerve become, precede, preclude the world itself. Space, to be space, is a surface against space. The eye, the breath, exist to extend the body, the surface, the space, the sealer, the limit of desire.

*r!*

After the very respects—

it being a wing-wing thing
a phosphorus shape, a pink

—to pieces of my Pa

I add
disruption

what a turnabout!
now my strange
is less regular sad
less conspiratorial

than

agitation

I am a value

let's I and I express *together*

Do we appreciate want?

What is reliable?

Together we cast the lead

     barbwire hook

     into the nesting pipe

the alphas filter
from on high

what expense, I—

*n*

# A Future of Glamour Unlike Any Previous Past

## Abstract

In the glamour hemisphere, if the looky is a sandalwood thing, then chiaroscuro charlatans will render mute nudes and catwalk neutrals. Blue next to green is a lessering equation. A single rule governs all glamour. Depending on the context, there is contrast drama. In conjunction with demonstrating lightness, there may arise difficulties in the visual system. The leaf is shown in three glamours: green, greener, and less. The map of veins says you are here at all hands on deck. You are here at the golden corral tipping your hat. You are here at the moonwalking blackbird, the diner at the hairpin turn. If glamour is scheming hot, then only filled with light does the vase become a vase, does the leaf become lookable. It is true that I may speak to no one. Least vulgar of us all the cutthroat glamours in the eddy with its sequins.

## Strip District Eclogue

no, there was beauty in the two girls
lying on the hood of the car

peeled mangoes down the city's throat
swallowed into a doomsday suspended

a river away     the molt of too many waterfowl
& men who can smell a girl's close call

with bridges     like a dog who can smell
cancer growing in a tit

## I will not sad-song the loss of solution

I had a sensation

The steroids weren't working to forget

Something like riding horseback through a pink forest

Or, just

Inflamed

It was a pink forest, you know

Like all things pink

They called it pink for a reason

It was a pink forest of deep things surrounded by forts

Fortitude

There were several artifacts

Indicating need for authorship

Vital organs

Tell-tale signs of predation

There were traces of children playing those games

The journeys of spiritual séance—

I went there once in a while

## Algorithm

fall's light coasted over
the prairie & I sat up humming
thought of getting a dog
how the cat would take it
my friend was having

a stroke in front of his
children & I don't know
anything about cat feelings
but why take the risk
if we were already happy
all of us like that

# Cruelty Is Not What One Believes it to Be

*Abstract*

From an evolutionary standpoint, creation favors the downsized. Take the nano processor. Its superscalar architecture executes more than one instruction at a time, the dual headed *Gee* and *Haw.* Taught to respond to signals and for powering grinding machines, a team of oxen, too, are intrinsically parallel. Though not a mythical creature, the mature ox possesses four stomachs. The walls of which are taut with mythical darkness. If *cruelty is sensation itself*, then as a true-horned ruminant the ox is happiest when it plows. The ox lives and dies in place, can be moved only by will or altered will. The year the coloreds are led to the flood the way my granddaddy led a tied sack of kittens to the river, the ox remained in place. In most cases, it is the field that moves beneath the ox. Trained since birth in the art of *draft animalia*, a team of oxen are oft "yoked in fate." Thus sure-footed, the ox proves forthcoming with mercy for the teamster whose cruelty is in his erection, his *Get up* and *Whoa.*

How many turnabout

& fix this whole

this now
) this fewer
is strange

of what erasure
do I remind myself

I stand
behind the fig leaf

a lasso lashing
rainstorm

curettage

the traces
of journeys

       that pass

I the rainstorm

where the lasso lashing
cuts the fig leaf
       vital sign
       of predation
       state of emergency
what they call the scything

I am not sure

of what I remind myself

Is heaven under that place

Is heaven firmness not composed

Is heaven colored

Is heaven without being able

The star is many and scissoring!

In any case
speaking briefly,

I failed the person
of most small love

On the destruction
that is complete—

what artifact
do I resemble

am I where
the blowings reach?

## Personal Science Tracing as a Bear in the Lake on the Sun

Given to gruff a little. Then the buff
of brazier. In the right light

it is lewdly believable that the fish morphed into little castles

and in this way, left the stream.

Several minds ago my physician drowned me in an existential void. To some it seemed
a drunk tank. *T* is for Trazodone. *T* is for twinkle.

To me all the daughters were danger. The brown one
swayed to her inside voices: *kill kill kill.* The white one was stuck on the nod.
I was the ursus unaware of the blood that spread from her seat.

*T* is for temporary. *T* is for timebomb. *T* is for the telling that has to end somewhere.

Blue is for the contrary bear

fishing the fish on the moon.

We understand adornment

We understand a decoration

actually

at the moment

this is all a point
of corruption

Anyhow—
simple


small love

small

you failed it

in person

*n*

## True Self Model in which the Mind Is a Container

There is an endless to be blacked out of my mind. Because the me
is meanly coddled, that I am perceived full of lies is not true. There is a booth inside my head
where me shimmies like a pump on a reel, a challenge to hands with no protective gear.
Because I am red and jealous every towel has a little strangle. A little movie.
Because the cum is cakey and rude exploded soda on the counter—like this I'd never
known. A heated goo that goes pop. The Christmas miracle. I'll stop
there. Because it's Chanel I lather it on like Chanel would want me
to. Some ideas just zap into my head! All over the scarlet map we plump
through the great state of dot to dot to stream. I try to lose her
in the weedy cutty corn, in the radon mine with the merry widows.
Because I am red and jealous I want to barrel and dump her. Zoom out
and there me is glib as a mineral soak, waist high in the nettles.

## Pastiche Eclogue

Is there any one sense in this thing
or is someone just poppin' corn?
This is not so totally an ugly. The heat
is never nice & the cloud, the could
now tuned with purple, gloves like a pass
over town. I come here occasionally

for the wow. I ask for sex because I like
the way it feels to do away with all the sexiness.
Too smart of me to put it any other way.
There is the necessity and then there is
the necessity. Off I go to the daughters
and the daughters' *blank*. I came for the long
wow in this thing. You there wolf as wolf hair.
You'll take it, all that is me. The junk
and the junkish.

Hungry Like Red

## [e.g. . . .]

in which we contemplate the cock, largely because it presents itself for contemplation through its natural business, its business of lengthening, in which we contemplate almost exclusively the corona of the cock, its glistening glans, its pinkness no matter what color, its pinkness that shines through as being only that swelling which needs our attention, in which we ignore the full topography of the cock, its layers and its canvasses, the acquaintancy and familiarity which can be achieved in exploring its exquisite folds, its ampallang—it is much more than "tab A into slot B"—there is its proximity to the cremaster muscle, the physiology of pleasure, in which we ignore the true length of the cock, ignore the bulb for the crown, that shattery which is given to us to sip, which he gives to us to sip, in which we then must praise the cock for being more than how he knows to give it, more than what we take into our mouths & pucker, must praise its grossly oversimplified eruptions, the titanic shadow it casts on the tongue, in which we must praise more than its propagation of seed, more than its biblical agenda—but the splendor of its musky thirst, its conversion so truthfully compelled.

[. . .]

## Illusion Is the Medium which Allows Emptiness to Become Something Special

### Abstract

For example: You are about to be attacked by a _____. It can rip your legs off. It has been following you through the _____, captivated by your light-reflecting sweat. You have a modicum of options. The first depends on your proximity to awareness—how long has it been following you? Does it look angry? Agitated? List the signs. Do it now. Don't jog back to that thought—your mother's quilt and the body under it. Is there really time for this? The hangnails of solipsism doing its bidding? In some cases you may have no choice but to fight. _____ may indicate imminent aggressiveness. Your survival depends on a crucial detail. Think: Your survival depends on past events. *Do not* _____. What was it? Something you read? Something you wrote? Know the odds of clouds in your favor. That one there looks to be a richly wrapped gift.

$r_4!$

I practice

the scissoring
          scheme

no more veiny
bundle

The insecurity of air

which is resent
            swallowed whole


            the sugar
            explodes with a sky of

Why talk scars

open under

I practice restlessness
then ease

under the open sky
of this

I always remind
myself
of what
              I erase

*n*

# New Scatology at a Crossroads

*Abstract*

It is counseled that a woman should not bleed alone in bear country, as a woman's scent tolls uninterrupted, as blood in the wood attracts the wild. All bears are big, but under most circumstances a bear's size is routinely misjudged. What colors a red apple red. Frosty nematodes. Fertilizer. A bear, too, wants to sleep the sleep of apples cuddled with wedges of snow. The suspected strongest of all mammals, a bear's tonnage is to lava pummel as cysts are to mammilla. Women are counseled not to bleed alone with bells while burying apples. What reddens a red apple red. I buried one part in a billion at Telephone Ridge. There is no interrupting a bear's size, as its attraction is often misjudged. Cuddled with wedges of snow, *Animalia chordata mammalia carnivora ursidae ursus americanus* sleeps the sleep of apples too.

# In the white world,

you hope it's not true, but every door is green.

Behind them histrionic syntax complicates

the money shot. Oooo cum wagging through the air.

Oooo marketing genius,

the miraculous garage is full of red Cadillacs.

There is a magazine for every question: *Several instructions*

*for timber-framing. Did the ancients know about catnip?*

A creature crawls from some dark place,

bites you in the leg, then crawls back.

*Did the ancients know about Pomeranians?*

Described as *canis pomeranus*, their tails often curl

over their backs, backs of German origin.

I'll marry in, then out. It is the feeling I had and still hold

for strolling under a sky so blue and visible and starred.

# A Village Life

We have preached this landscape

where everything is incorporated

and telephoned. This is the machine gun villa.

A million models are priced, tagged,

and ready to ship

from the warehouse of our machine gun villa.

Maple syrup, moccasins, Mount Rushmore key chains,

potato guns *a-ratatatatting* in the machine gun villa.

As for the rising of ideas, I love your tan

little miss river rat. Go further and it is further

into the machine

gun villa. A rose on a slab of bloodbath?

& not a tidbit of hostility for the machine gun

villa.  I love the river of your solar burn.

Yizzerd!  What beautiful country the machine gun villa.

## Dream City Eclogue

the last time we are touching
you are wearing leather
in the Beckham (woman) haircut
I almost tell you about the red-
head but the fan blades chop
the air too loud and thickly

my skin no our skin sparkles
sparkles like it's inlaid with gold
you laugh and say someone wanted
the streets to look pretty
I give you a long last hug & order
a slice from the cake made of air

# Animals Do Not Commit Delusional Acts

*Abstract*

Compared to an egg, seashell, or shark, humans are in general and already, crazy. Only the human looks away when attacked, though its propensity to do so exponentially increases the probability for loss of life. The human turns inward, protects the eyes by turning to the cave and its shadows. Only the human believes in the body of shadow, in the premise of its actions based on the actions of other humans and their shadows. The human can cut its own throat. It can seek without hunger. The animal realm is that of *being-to-being.* Never over or under done. Only the human says, *sorry crab, sorry goose,* to a thing that's killed. Only humans smile for pictures and grow concerned over their proximity to lightning, concerned that the moon over the kill is too contrived. Humans miss their mothers. Replace their teeth. Invent human death in all ways ungracious. Only humans practice to film it. Animals do not commit such delusional acts. Thus the human puts its baby human in a baby carriage and pushes it away.

*r*

at intervals never when the moon is blue
I buzz to be trim & trussed



Barring
at any time
do we like that
Like that
in which
always we like it

Hindmost
I buzz for it

Whatever piece
portion
shape I canvass
from Pa

I annex

I utter I am a merit
together we appreciate what's
bona fide

       Together we fathom
the latticework
In the lair     In the
flue

The seepage alphas
from there, aloft

for me I charge

I stand
in need of a fig leaf with the sweep of a lasso

Heaven firmly there

astral blah
the snip of keepsakes

Aside this what's-been-set-down
you'd consider
I hadn't been cherished—

that in any case
that in a nutshell
I failed a little darling

Within reach
the raze breezes in

We understand motif

Presently a spot of taint

We who can
why don't we make it
where we love it

On the wind
with the bang of sugar

# notes

*r!* describes how many ways a certain set of r can be combined.

"Dialogical Repose" is inspired by Ruth Ellen Kocher and Anne Marie Rooney.

"Pastiche Eclogue" includes a line spoken by Carolina, Group F, CC 2010.

"Dream City Eclogue" is for Anne Marie Rooney.

The phrase "machine gun villa" was inspired by a conversation with Lawrence Raab.

"Algorithm" is for Steve Davenport.

"The Organism is Escaping" paraphrases sections of Deleuze's *Francis Bacon: The Logic of Sensation.*

"Cruelty is Not What One Believes it to Be" and "Animals Do Not Commit Delusional Acts" quote artist Yun Jeong Hong.

In "New Scatalogy at a Crossroads" the phrase "sleep the sleep of apples" is from Frederico Garcia Lorca's "Gacela of the Dark Death."

# biographical note

Lillian-Yvonne Bertram is a 2014 recipient of a National Endowment for the Arts Creative Writing Poetry Fellowship. Her first book, *But a Storm is Blowing From Paradise*, was selected by Claudia Rankine as the 2010 Benjamin Saltman Award winner and published by Red Hen Press in 2012. Her chapbook, *cutthroat glamours*, was published by Phantom Books in 2013. Her works have appeared in *Black Warrior Review*, *Callaloo*, *Cream City Review*, *Court Green*, *DIAGRAM*, *Gulf Coast*, *Harvard Review*, *Indiana Review*, *jubilat*, *Mid-American Review*, *Narrative Magazine*, *OH NO*, *Saltfront*, *Subtropics*, *Sou'wester*, *Tupelo Quarterly*, and more. She holds a PhD in creative writing from the University of Utah.

CPSIA information can be obtained
at www.ICGtesting.com
Printed in the USA
LVOW09s0047250418
574789LV00003B/92/P